4/00

P9-DTB-745

DARWINISM

TODAY

NEANDERTHALS, BANDITS AND FARMERS

HOW AGRICULTURE REALLY BEGAN

Colin Tudge

Yale University Press
New Haven and London

Published 1998 in Great Britain by Weidenfeld & Nicolson.
Published in the United States 1999 by Yale University Press.
Copyright © 1998 by Colin Tudge.
Foreword copyright © 1998 by Helena Cronin and Oliver Curry.
All rights reserved.
This book may not be reproduced, in whole or in part, including
illustrations, in any form (beyond that copying permitted by Sections
107 and 108 of the U.S. Copyright Law and except by reviewers for
the public press), without written permission from the publishers.

Printed in the United States of America.

Library of Congress Cataloging-in-Publication Data:

Tudge, Colin.
    Neanderthals, bandits and farmers : how agriculture really
began / Colin Tudge.
       p.   cm.
    Reprint. Originally published : London : Weidenfeld &
Nicolson, c1998.
    Includes bibliographical references.
    ISBN 0-300-08024-7 (cloth : alk. paper)
    1. Agriculture—Origin. 2. Neolithic period. I. Title. II. Title:
How agriculture really began.
GN799.A4T83   1999
630'.9'01—dc21   99–15178
                                             CIP

A catalogue record for this book is available from the British Library.

The paper in this book meets the guidelines for permanence and
durability of the Committee on Production Guidelines for Book
Longevity of the Council on Library Resources.

10   9   8   7   6   5   4   3   2   1

630.9
TuD
1999

CONTENTS

....

The Series Editors thank
Peter Tallack and
Robert G. Kruszynski
for their help.

FOREWORD

Darwinism Today is a series of short books by leading figures in the field of evolutionary theory. Each title is an authoritative pocket introduction to the Darwinian ideas that are setting today's intellectual agenda.

The series developed out of the Darwin@LSE programme at the London School of Economics. The Darwin Seminars provide a platform for distinguished evolutionists to present the latest Darwinian thinking and to explore its application to humans. The programme is having an enormous impact, both in helping to popularize evolutionary theory and in fostering cross-disciplinary approaches to shared problems.

With the publication of **Darwinism Today** we hope that the best of the new Darwinian ideas will reach an even wider audience.

Helena Cronin and Oliver Curry
Series Editors

DARWIN@

NEANDERTHALS, BANDITS AND FARMERS

HOW AGRICULTURE REALLY BEGAN

INTRODUCTION

Tradition has it that agriculture began in the Middle East around 10,000 years ago and so created the 'Neolithic Revolution' with farming itself accompanied by the first traces of cities, and soon, great leaps in the variety and subtlety of stone tools. And, so the story goes, once people realized the advantages and indeed the joys of farming, its skills spread rapidly to the furthest outposts of the world. The old hunting-gathering lifestyle that had prevailed for the previous few million years – the daring men hunting and the patient women gathering – suddenly began to seem both dangerous and precarious. People worldwide abandoned the ancient ways as soon as news spread of better things.

This view of agricultural history is forgivable, for this is what the archaeological record seems to show. Before about 10,000 years ago there are virtually no signs of plant cultivation or animal domestication anywhere in the world. After, there are clear indications of both at several sites in the Middle East, such as Jericho on the West Bank of the Jordan and Catal Huyuk in Turkey; and later, at intervals of a few thousand years, obvious signs of farming appear in the Indus Valley, in China and in several locations in the Americas. Such are the perceived advantages of agriculture that the only apparent difficulty is to explain how the idea of farming could have travelled from one community to another. Did the word spread while the people stayed still, like a sound-wave through a cymbal? Did groups of farmers sally forth, bearing the word, like Neolithic freelance consultants? Or was it that farming was an evolutionary stage, a stage that people were predestined to attain sooner or later? This last idea appealed to late and post-Victorian scholars who were still anxious to reconcile the notion of Charles Darwin (1809–82) that human beings are evolved animals, with the story of Genesis, which holds that God created us and controls our destiny. To be sure we evolve but – the conceit had it – we evolve along prescribed lines, step by step, steadily and inevitably becoming more like, well, Western scholars. That the first clear signs of agriculture are found in the Middle East is as it should be, since we trace our own cultural origins back to the ancient Jews and Greeks – who naturally would have been the first to dip their toes into the waters of civilization.

This, then, is the traditional view. But more and more scholars have become discontented with it, for all kinds of reasons. Many have pointed out that farming in Neolithic times was obviously harsh: that the first farming peoples were less robust than the hunter-gatherers who had preceded them, and suffered nutritional, traumatic and infectious disorders that their forebears had been spared. Why should it not be so? For one thing, hunter-gatherers clearly had a varied diet that included scores of different plants while farmers were commonly confined to just a few staple crops that sometimes failed and must often have been mouldy – just as is true of modern crops if not treated with fungicide, whether in the field or in store. The real problem, then, is not to explain why some people were slow to adopt agriculture but why anybody took it up at all when it was so obviously beastly.

With such thoughts in mind many scholars now suggest that, for thousands of years before the Neolithic farming revolution, human beings were already managing their environment to a greater or lesser extent. They were not simply hunting and gathering, but also coercing their prey to behave more amenably, and perhaps encouraging favoured plants. Dramatic as they appear, then, the changes of the Neolithic Revolution were not really revolutionary, but merely a consolidation of established trends. People did not invent agriculture and shout for joy; they drifted or were forced into it, protesting all the way.

In this small book I want to take this line of thinking much further. I want to argue that from at least 40,000 years ago – the late Palaeolithic – people were managing their environment to such an extent that they can properly be called 'proto-farmers'. In the light of this idea much that is otherwise mysterious falls easily into place. It helps to explain the enormous ecological success of human beings after that time – for this is when they spread out of Eurasia (where they had long since spread from Africa) and into Australia, the Pacific, and the Americas. It may also help to explain why, as our late Paleolithic and more recent ancestors travelled, they killed so many animals in their way – the mammoths are just one example among scores of others. Part-time proto-farmers may even have delivered the *coup de grâce* to the Neanderthals who obdurately remained as hunters.

Finally, of course, if farming – or 'proto-farming' – is truly ancient, then it becomes quite unnecessary to explain how or why agriculture apparently spread from the Middle East to the East and to the Americas in the millennia after the Neolithic Revolution. For it didn't spread at all. Everyone in all of those locations knew how to farm even before they got there. At different places at different times and for different (but always related) reasons, people settled down to farming in particular spots over long periods of time on a scale that is large enough to show up in the archaeological record. Only operations that are already large-scale are liable to leave any trace at all.

The hypothesis is, in short, that by the time of the Neolithic Revolution, farming was already an ancient and established set of crafts; and that the carnage wrought by late Paleolithic people is best understood if we perceive them as proto-farmers. This is indeed only a hypothesis: for reasons that will become apparent, the direct evidence is scant. The role of hypotheses, however, is to help us to look at the evidence afresh.

First of all, then, what is agriculture? What are we trying to explain?

....

CHAPTER I

The Several Faces of Agriculture

Hunters and gatherers, at their most basic, simply take and consume what the environment has to offer – whatever components of the wild environment happen to be available and consumable. Farmers seek to influence the environment, to manipulate it, in ways that increase the amount of food that is available and consumable. That is the essence of it. In practice this general tendency to manipulate the environment, and so to increase its amenability and productivity, has developed into three quite different kinds of activity.

The first of these is horticulture (from the Latin *hortus* meaning garden): growing food plants intensively, initially on an individual basis. Gardening is its basic form even though horticulture nowadays employs many arable techniques. Horticulture can produce a lot of good food in small spaces, but is extremely labour intensive. We can envisage plantations and orchards – of olives, vines, apples, or whatever – as extensions of horticulture.

The second method of manipulating the environment is arable farming. What really differentiates arable farming from horticulture is ploughing: breaking the soil in an entire field as a preliminary, removing the natural flora, and beginning with a *tabula rasa*. Horticulture in its pristine form does not require this; at its simplest it merely involves shoving a stick in the ground – not a seed but a cutting. Arable farming on a modern scale could not truly begin until people started using animal power, although many people – including all the pre-European American farmers – ploughed the soil with digging tools, without the aid of animal power. (Strictly speaking only arable farming should be called 'agriculture' since this literally means – in modified Latin – 'cultivation of the fields'.) Arable farming produces staple crops on the large scale, such as cereals and potatoes. Pulses are also grown on an arable scale these days, although traditionally they are the province of the horticulturalist, as in the English gardener's row of broad beans (of the genus *Vicia*) and the Aztec's kidney beans (genus *Phaseolus*).

The third form of farming is pastoral. Traditionally, people simply allowed their herds to graze or sometimes to browse on natural herbage; the ground was not ploughed or even fertilized except by the animals' own manure. Nowadays, of course, in rich countries, grassland is created by ploughing and then sowing custom-bred, 'improved' grasses, so that intensive pastoralism becomes an extension of arable farming. And of course intensive livestock is now largely or entirely fattened on grain produced by arable techniques. But pastoral farming traditionally took the natural vegetation as it was; and even in modern Britain, where farming is high-tech, sheep and cattle in the uplands are still set to graze on whatever is growing locally.

So under the broad banner of 'farming' there are three very different kinds of activity. Because they are so different there has, traditionally, been rivalry and conflict between them. Indeed, this rivalry is a powerful literary thread that runs from the Old Testament to Western 'B movies'.

'The farmers and the ranchers should be friends'

Many of us of a certain generation have an idealized picture of agriculture rooted somewhere in the English Home Counties *circa* 1955, in which arable and pastoral farming were happily integrated in what were (and are) called 'mixed farms'. Cereals were grown for a few years on favoured fields and then livestock was introduced for a year or two to restore the fertility. Sheep were fed on 'catch crops' of autumn turnips, and chickens on tail-corn, while pigs fed on surplus whey as milk was turned into butter. It was all very cosy and logical – and in principle unimprovable. The idea was ancient – essentially eighteenth-century; medieval farmers followed much the same principles although such systems could not work to best advantage until the land was properly enclosed, with fences, walls and hedges. The 1950s truly saw the flowering of the mixed farm: ancient practice was brought to fruition by post-war zeal and modern techniques (notably the tractor, which is many times more powerful than the horse and consumes only when it works).

But in much of the world through most of history arablists and pastoralists have been in conflict, often mortal. After all, they practise very different kinds of activity which, except in highly controlled circumstances, are an 'either or'. Traditional pastoralists prefer to leave the wild vegetation as it is while arablists begin by getting rid of it; and since arablists must choose the most fertile spots the pastoralists are inevitably marginalized. Furthermore – and this is crucial – pastoralists are bound to shift around, at least from valley to upland as the seasons change and often from district to district, nomadically. But arablists prefer to stay in the same place. They cannot afford to invest huge amounts of work in a field and then just walk away from it.

The conflict between the arablists and the pastoralists is a common theme of Western movies, as reflected in the song from *Oklahoma!*: 'O, the farmers and the ranchers should be friends . . .' In this context 'farmer' specifically means 'arablist', and a rancher is a particular kind of pastoralist. The story suggests, *inter alia*, that they had hitherto been sworn enemies.

This is also a common biblical theme, as in the story

of Cain and Abel. Note that Abel was the 'keeper of sheep' while Cain was 'a tiller of the ground' (Genesis 4:2). There is a pleasant irony in this. I remember in the post-hippy 1970s that many who were advocating vegetarianism were apt to offer Cain and Abel as a morality tale – but this obliged them to invert the story and so to suggest that Abel, the gentle victim, was the vegetarian while Cain, the bloody-handed murderer, was the archetypal carnivore. Harold McGee's book *On Food and Cooking*, which made a great impact in the 1980s, perpetuated this myth. If anyone had referred to the text they would have seen that Cain was the vegetarian. Note, too, that the quarrel began when each of the brothers offered the fruits of his labours – lambs or corn – to God: 'And the Lord had respect unto Abel and to his offering. But unto Cain and to his offering he had not respect.'

Most of the Bible is about agriculture and it seems to me that, in general, it gives the pastoralists a much better press than the arablists. Arable farming in Egypt as depicted in Exodus is literal slavery. When Jesus is born he is attended by shepherds; nobody brings any sheaves of wheat. But then, in biblical times, arable farming would have been considered far more 'aggressive' than pastoralism because it has a far greater immediate impact on the environment. To be sure, grazing and browsing livestock do transform the local flora, and may do so quite quickly. But pastoralism is not immediately invasive; if the ground is not overgrazed then pleasant meadows are produced – again commonly conceived as idyllic – which can last indefinitely, millennium after millennium. Arable farming in contrast tends to degrade the soil quite quickly – except in favoured circumstances, with plenty of added manure. Arable farming, then, threatened traditional ways of life and, through its assertiveness – the way it disrupts the natural, 'God-given' landscape – it verged on blasphemy.

Thus the grand concept of farming breaks into three contrasting (and only sometimes complementary) approaches – horticulture, arable farming and pastoralism – of which some are more interventionist than others. Nevertheless, all of them – especially in comparison with modern agriculture – would at first have involved only a gentle series of interventions.

The prehistory of farming

Nowadays, farmers follow 'systems' in which many different activities are seamlessly integrated: so seamlessly, that we can easily overlook their multifariousness. Note how many separate activities are involved even in cultivating a single plant: preparation of the soil; breeding; propagation; crop protection; harvesting; perhaps storage. But note, too, that although modern farming involves all of these things as a matter of course, *any one of them taken alone* would make a difference.

This is crucial to the concept of 'proto-farming'. The first farmers – proto-farmers – did not devise all the techniques of farming simultaneously, and still less did they integrate them immediately into a system. Instead they adopted aspects of the whole piecemeal, one thing here and another somewhere else, at times abandoning one or another, but eventually bringing them all together. Furthermore, the inputs that now seem naturally to be first on the list of desiderata – plant breeding and soil preparation – were, almost undoubtedly, among the last to appear. The things that modern farmers undertake late in the cycle of cultivation – notably crop protection – were historically the earliest. With such thoughts in mind we can see how the skills of proto-farming arose, and finally came together.

Plant protection and propagation

Crop protection at its simplest need involve nothing more than driving away rivals from some favoured plant, like a wild nut tree. Many animals do this. Ants drive other insects away from coveted acacia trees. Fish drive other grazers away from favoured patches of algae on the coral reef. Chimps drive away rival chimps. And so on. At its lowest level, crop protection is an aspect of territoriality. We need not doubt that early hunting-gathering people drove away all threats, as far as they could, from fruitful groves.

Weeding, pulling out rival plants that threaten to choke the favoured one, is a natural extension of this. Pruning and even dead-heading follow soon after. Woolly monkeys have been reported to remove dead branches from trees.

Such basic care is rudimentary indeed, but it makes a

huge difference. Over time – and not much time – such protection can have profound effects on the genetics of the favoured plants (or animals). Thus plants that enjoy protection from some special predator do not have to be as toxic or spiky as plants that are not so protected. Since it is physiologically expensive to produce toxins or spikes, natural selection would favour those that were less toxic or spiky if there were no need for them to be so; and those that expend less energy on defence have more to spare for growth. At the same time, particular animals gear themselves more and more to their favoured food plant.

Many creatures help also to propagate the plants they feed upon. Indeed many plants rely upon the animals that eat them to disperse their seeds, fruit or other propagules. Fleshy fruits have clearly co-evolved with the animals that spread them. Forests in Borneo and Sumatra lose many species of tree when orang-utans disappear because the orangs spread their seeds. Removal of fruit bats in many areas of the world has the same effect. We can envisage that early hominids, newly bipedal, would have used their liberated hands for carrying, and would surely have carried fruits from place to place – conveniently disseminating the seed as they went.

Note, too, that many crops can be grown without spreading specific propagules. Thus it is often possible to grow a new tree simply by thrusting a stick into the ground. This is all too easy with willows in Britain, and even easier with a great many trees in the palm-house conditions of the tropics. In short, we can imagine the first horticulturalists – proto-horticulturalists – spreading their favourite food trees just by placing a few sticks around the place. We can imagine, too, that they may often have created coppices where they intended only to make fences, perhaps to keep the pigs at bay.

Even these very simple acts – crop protection and passive propagation – would have made a profound difference to the survival of the early hominids. And these simple acts are serious components of farming. Note how much effort still goes in to the repulsion of pests and the suppression of weeds, and of course into propagation.

The beginnings of game management

Game management means exerting some control over other species without thoroughly domesticating them. Again, some animals act as 'game managers' of a kind. Ants, for example, marshal semi-wild flocks of aphids – greenfly – to 'milk' the sweet honeydew, the surplus sugar, that they excrete. And there are human antecedents of game management. There is evidence from North America – for example, in Badlands, South Dakota – of native Americans chasing bison over cliffs, presumably as an easy source of meat or hide. It is a small step from there to corralling.

Fire can also be used to manage game. Many have asked why Australian aborigines apparently do not farm – to which Rhys Jones, an anthropologist at the Australian

National University at Canberra provides a simple answer: They do! They practise what he calls 'firestick farming'. Much of Australia is covered by grass; grass blades grow from the base so unless the tops are removed the grass becomes rank. Hence one way to manage grassland is to burn it: remove the surplus dead stuff, and allow the young leaves to come through from beneath. Farmers do this worldwide. Australian aborigines have clearly been burning the bush in a very orderly fashion for tens of thousands of years – freshening the vegetation by setting fire to it, and so creating patches of green. Small rodents and marsupials that are already in residence (and stay in their holes while the fires pass over) then breed rapidly, and larger grazing animals like kangaroos come hopping in. Then the aborigines can feast. Thus they not only influence the behaviour of animals – prompting them to move from place to place – but also increase their biomass, by providing the extra food they need to breed. Human beings had some control of fire at least 500,000 years ago. If modern Australian aborigines are anything to go by – and they probably are – fire has played an enormous role in our success, not only as an aid to cooking (which broadens the range of food available to us) but also in game management. Game management is very significant proto-pastoralism.

So when did farming really begin?

If we accept that human beings and their closest extinct relatives – collectively known as 'hominids' – had *always* been 'farming', in the sense that they were manipulating the plants and animals around them in ways that increased their own efficiency as hunters and gatherers, then the real issue is when they became aware that they were doing these things, and started to do them consciously and deliberately. Whenever palaeo-anthropologists want to say that hominids first became 'conscious', in a modern sense, then I am content to say, 'That is when farming began'.

It seems that human beings of the genus *Homo* first appeared around two million years ago. And the first anatomically human beings – people who would have looked perfectly at home in a bus queue – appeared on this Earth something over 100,000 years ago in Africa. But the first anatomically modern humans seem to have made the same kinds of tools and did the same kinds of things with them as their more brutish-looking antecedents had been doing for a million years. The first people that really seem to impress the palaeo-anthropologists are those of the late Palaeolithic, of around 40,000 years ago. These people apparently started to innovate. They began producing a greater range of tools and refining the designs, and they began serious cave-painting, which quickly reached a very high standard. This seems to represent a shift in consciousness – deliberate innovation, and not just a tendency to do whatever was done by the generation before. And it seems reasonable to me to suggest, in the same somewhat arbitrary but nonetheless reasonable spirit, that the first bona fide farmers – or at least proto-farmers – appeared at this time too. It is not that this is when they began doing the things that we can call 'farming'. Rather, this is the time when they became fully aware that they were farming. The somewhat hit-and-miss effects that they had upon their environment graduated into a series of conscious and deliberate manipulations, albeit founded on a rule-of-thumb approach and often ritualistic, as indeed farming still is.

The point is not to put a precise date on this transition, but to note that human beings virtually throughout their two million year history have not merely been 'hunters and gatherers', in the way that these terms are generally understood but have always manipulated their environment in various ways that increased their food supply.

The next part of the hypothesis is that farming even in its 'proto-' state – an *ad hoc* collection of activities that coaxes more food from the environment – has an enormous impact on the ecological success of those who practise it, while severely subverting other people or other species who do not practise it. And as we shall see, the hypothesis that people first consciously began farming 40,000 years ago seems to mesh with a number of other significant observations.

....

The End of the Neanderthals and the Pleistocene Overkill

I do not envisage that late Palaeolithic proto-farmers were full-time farmers. Of course they were not. I envisage merely that they practised some degree of environmental manipulation – crop protection and prop-agation, and game management – in addition to their hunting and gathering. Proto-farming for them was virtually a hobby, a kind of back-up. Neither do I imagine any kind of uniformity. I would guess that some people 'farmed' – *sensu lato* – some of the time and not at others, in some places and not at others, and that some people farmed a lot, and some not at all. And we need not assume that people who have the skills of pastoralism necessarily abandon hunting in its favour. The Hottentot people of south-west Africa, for example, were known until recently to keep goats for a few years at a time and then, when it suited them, to get rid of the goats and revert to hunting. They may have been following such a pattern for many centuries. The hypothesis is, nonetheless, that a small amount of hobby proto-farming would have a huge and disproportionate influence on ecological success.

In the harsh conditions of the wild all animals live on the edge of disaster. Specifically, animals that live by hunting whatever is around, or grazing or browsing the wild vegetation, have to move to where the food is; and when the food supply fails, as it is bound to do at some seasons of the year or over periods of years when the climate takes a turn for the worse, the animals must either tough it out by starvation or dormancy, or move out, or die. But a creature that can manipulate the environment even ever so slightly can hang on in a given location when the more passive creatures are obliged to move out. Over the creature's whole range, this ability to hang on just a little better in particular locations even when times are bad means that the total population is just a little higher than it would be if the creature was *simply* a hunter and *simply* a gatherer of wild plants.

Then again – and this is crucial – an animal that farms for a hobby can become a far more effective and ultimately devastating hunter than one that merely hunts!

A moment's reflection shows why this is so. A population of predators that relies entirely upon hunting is dependent upon the population of its prey species. The classic ecological example, in every textbook, is that of the northern lynx, which feeds upon the snow-shoe hare. The hares are locked into a cycle of boom and bust that depends upon their relationship with their food plants: the hares are the predators of the plants and their population waxes and wanes depending on the state of the vegetation. But the fate of the lynxes is linked to that of the hares. As the hare population rises and plummets, so too, even more dramatically, does that of the lynxes.

Predators that have a broader prey base can to some extent avoid such peaks and troughs. As one prey species becomes rare they switch to another, just as sea-otters switch to sea-urchins when clams become rare. Omnivores like human beings have an even greater advantage: when the meat supply fails they can get by on plants, at least for a time.

But creatures that also farm for a hobby have a triple advantage. Their existence ceases to depend upon the wild fauna at all. Because this is so, their population need not decrease just because one particular prey species becomes rare. Today, suburban domestic cats provide the perfect model. They are sustained by Kit-e-Kat and Whiskas, and remain thick on the ground even when the local song-birds and mice decline. Hence they remain a predatory force long after the prey species have become extremely rare. For prey animals in a state of nature rarity is a refuge. But when the predator has a secure, independent food base, mere scarcity is no longer protective.

Many anthropologists have argued, too, that people

ALBUQUERQUE ACADEMY LIBRARY

do not hunt only for food. Male status or display could play a large part too. Indeed, many predatory animals, not just humans, demonstrate their prowess by killing. Many male birds, for example, seek to attract mates by presenting the female with some matted corpse. We can imagine human hunters seeking to impress potential mates – or indeed to impress their whole tribe – by some special feat of killing. We can also imagine that the kudos would be even greater if the hunter came back with the head of some creature – especially a big or dangerous one – that everyone knew to be rare or especially difficult to catch. Human males might thus make a virtue of hunting to extinction.

In short, we can envisage that human beings who supplemented their own survival by farming, albeit on a small scale, could easily drive other species into oblivion, perhaps by hunting them even more vigorously after they had become rare. A full-time hunter is unable to do this. The full-time hunter is liable to die out as prey becomes scarce.

Now, it seems virtually certain that all the main grades of hominid arose in Africa. *Ardipithecus* appeared in Africa about five million years ago, *Australopithecus* a little later. The first *Homo* in the form of *Homo habilis* appeared more than two million years ago. *Homo erectus* appeared about two million years ago and was the first hominid to migrate out of Africa, perhaps around 1.5 million years ago. Around the same time *Homo ergaster* appeared, who was perhaps the ancestor of later humans; *Homo heidelbergensis*, formerly known as 'archaic *Homo sapiens*', who also migrated out of Africa, perhaps about half a million years ago, was the ancestor both of *Homo neanderthalensis* and of *Homo sapiens*; and *Homo sapiens* first appeared in anatomically modern form around 100,000 years ago. But around 40,000 years ago, in late Palaeolithic times, the migrations became even more impressive, as people learnt to build boats and crossed the open sea. Thus around 40,000 years ago people entered Australia for the first time, from South East Asia, and by at least 30,000 years ago had begun to populate Pacific islands. Around 13,000 years ago people first entered the Americas – not in fact by sailing, but by walking across the land bridge commonly referred to as Beringia, which formed between Siberia and Alaska during Ice Ages, when the sea level fell by up to 200 metres.

It is now clear that very soon after human beings entered these land masses for the first time, the local fauna began to go extinct, with the bigger animals suffering most. Thus Australia lost thirteen genera of large animals after 40,000 years ago, including giant kangaroos, a giant horned tortoise, and the rhino-sized wombat relatives called diprotodonts (which may have given rise to the myth of the 'bunyip', an Antipodean bogeyman used to scare Australian children), plus the marsupial 'lion' (*Thylacoleo*) which preyed upon them. In the centuries immediately after the first human beings arrived in North America around 13,000 years ago, no fewer than thirty-three out of forty-five genera of large mammals disappeared. These included camels, giant beavers, peccaries (American pigs), several types of elephant including mammoths and mastodonts, giant ground sloths and the glyptodont – which was an armadillo the size of a bread van – plus the animals that preyed on them: sabre-toothed cats, dire wolves, and giant running bears. In modern-day North America the large fauna consists of just a few deer (wapiti, moose, white-tailed deer and mule deer); bison, which for a few thousand years were as common as mice; and just a few others, such as mountain goats and bighorn sheep. These creatures do well because there is no longer any competition from camels, ground sloths, mammoths and so on; and because each of them has some special quality that made them particularly difficult to destroy. For example, moose and bighorn sheep both live in remote places (deep northern forests or high mountains) while wild bison make unpredictable migrations over great distances.

South America's large animals suffered even more a couple of millennia later as the human beings spread down from the north; within a few centuries, forty-six genera were lost out of fifty-eight. Two distinct orders of hoofed animal, including the genera *Macrauchenia*, which looked like large camels with a short trunk, and *Toxodon*, which looked like hippo-sized guinea pigs, were lost forever. The pattern is repeated worldwide: Madagascar lost its giant tortoises, hippos, lemurs, and elephant birds when people arrived at about the time of Christ. (Elephant birds were like giant emus. They were the heaviest birds that ever lived, and laid the biggest eggs of any creature – even bigger than any known dinosaur egg. Elephant birds may have given rise to the myth of the Roc which features in the tales of Sinbad.) When the Maoris arrived in New Zealand around the tenth century AD, the ecology was dominated by about fifteen species of moas, ostrich-like birds that ranged in size from that of a turkey to about eight feet tall – the tallest birds that ever lived and among the heaviest. Within a few centuries of the Maoris' arrival, the moas were gone.

The evidence now suggests that human hunters – not climate, as was formerly supposed – wiped out the large fauna. If climate were responsible, then we would expect the small animals to suffer even more than the large, yet in most cases the small animals remained virtually unscathed. Mice and shrews are vulnerable to changes in the climate because they are small but they are safe from predation by human beings. Besides, there is little independent evidence of a climate change that could account for such a die-out. Thus the first waves of destruction in Australia and the Americas are known as the Pleistocene overkill, and the Madagascan and New Zealand (and Hawaiian and many more) waves of destruction can be seen as part of the same process even though they occurred in more recent times. In general, the big herbivores and the big predators seemed to disappear more or less simultaneously – predators that included sabre-toothed cats and giant running bears in North America, and a giant short-winged eagle that preyed upon moas in New Zealand. We can reasonably assume that the big herbivores went extinct because they were targeted, and the big predators went because their prey base disappeared.

It makes sense, therefore, to argue that human hunters, not climate, killed the large animals of the Americas and Australia. Unlike the animals of Africa, which had spent two million years in the company of human beings, or those of Eurasia, which had experienced human beings over half-a-million years, the creatures of the Americas and Australia were totally unused to human ways: to the hunters who sometimes descended in a howling mob, and sometimes employed stealth, and always seemed to know where best to hide and – crucially – were able to strike at a distance with missiles such as stones, spears, and javelins.

But the argument makes even more sense if we suppose that the first people in the Americas and Australia were also manipulating the environment; that they were hobby farmers. If they were hobby farmers then, as I have argued, they would have been even more destructive predators. They could easily, and perhaps gleefully, have pursued the more spectacular creatures to extinction.

In other words, I suggest that some degree of farming helped to underpin the Pleistocene overkill – and indeed makes it more plausible.

Whatever happened to the Neanderthals?

We can use the same idea to explain an even more striking mystery. We know that our own ancestors – recognizably modern people and traditionally known as Cro-Magnons – were making their mark in Europe around 40,000 years ago. We also know that the Nean-derthals hung on in Europe until at least 35,000 years ago, and perhaps even until 27,000 years ago: so the two species of human lived side by side for at least 5,000 years and perhaps for more than 10,000 years.

Some have suggested direct conflict between the Cro-Magnons and the Neanderthals, as William Golding did in his novel *The Inheritors*. But if such conflict was common it is hard to see how the two human species could have co-existed for so long. Some have suggested in a rather vague way that the Neanderthals were romantic moon-worshippers, while the Cro-Magnons were more down-to-earth and practical, as psychologist Stan Gooch argues in his book of the late 1970s – it was a very seventies' book – *Guardians of the Ancient Wisdom*. This portrays the conflict as a kind of Palaeolithic rehearsal of the later conflict between the Dionysian and Apollonian traditions of Greece, or the Romantic and Classical traditions of Western culture in general.

In fact, Stan Gooch may be near to the mark, though not quite in the way he intended. Thus Clive Gamble, a palaeo-anthropologist at the University of Southampton, has suggested that the Cro-Magnons were indeed more down-to-earth, and that their practicality was expressed by improvements in hunting strategy. The Cro-Mag-nons, he suggests, got to know the habits of the animals they hunted and knew where to lie in wait; and different bands shared information, so that hunting parties could be forewarned of migrations days in advance. (I like to imagine that they communicated by beacon fires: after all, the people we used to call 'Red Indians' in North America used smoke signals until well into recent times, and they came originally from Eurasia. Perhaps the early native Americans brought to the prairies the skills they had developed on the steppes.) Most importantly of all Gamble suggests that the Cro-Magnons co-operated: that they traded tools – for which there is abundant evidence – and also traded information. Thus he suggests that the age of trade (and of information) is exceedingly ancient. This chimes too with the thesis of Matt Ridley's excellent book *The Origins of Virtue*: that human beings are innately co-operative creatures, and have indeed been trading since ancient times.

Well, I would just like to add to Clive Gamble's notion the idea that the improved foraging strategy of the Cro-Magnons included proto-farming, deliberate manipulation of the environment to coax more food from it. The Cro-Magnons did not only anticipate the presence of game. To a large extent they controlled it, encouraging the animals to congregate in some places rather than others. They further enhanced their own chances of survival by protecting and propagating favoured food plants. They would not have had to do much of this. Just a little could make all the difference.

So the clash between the Cro-Magnons and the Neanderthals was not merely one of efficient hunters versus inefficient hunters. It would have contained a crucial new element – of farmer versus hunter. In part the point is that the farmers are more efficient than the hunters, and produce more food, and reproduce more effectively. But in part, too, the hunters disappear because the farmers erode their prey base in the same way, as already suggested, the earliest North Americans' attacks upon the mammoths undermined the sabre-toothed cats.

Farmers and bandits

The clash of proto-farming Cro-Magnons with wild, predatory Neanderthals is again of the kind that has echoed through the ages, and is a favourite leitmotiv of the movies, particularly Westerns. Thus in Westerns the farmers are generally perceived as sad put-upons who are preyed on by bandits. Typically the farmers are Mexican, with suitably lugubrious moustaches. *The Seven Samurai* was a high-class 'Eastern', re-made as a high-class Western in *The Magnificent Seven*. The bandits are romantic figures, given to boozing, wenching, riding horses at high speed and firing their pistols for no particular reason. Well, this is one version of Romanticism. The bandits give the farmers a very hard time. But in the end the farmers win. The fight is not to the spectacular, but to the dogged. The descendants of the hand-wringing farmers of the movies are now driving Landrovers, or their American and Japanese equivalents, while the bandits have left no descendants at all because they were all hanged, or slaughtered in some climactic shoot-out.

I do not actually envisage that the clash between Cro-Magnons and Neanderthals took this literal form – we need not suppose that the Neanderthals lived as bandits

– but I do see a symbolic similarity. The bandits, like the Neanderthals, lived on their wits and took from the environment only what the environment had to offer. They were flashy, but they were always dependants. The farmers on the other hand, like the Cro-Magnons, sought to manipulate the environment so that it would produce – or 'bring forth' as the Old Testament is wont to say – the things they wanted. The farmers were dull by comparison, but they were in control.

But if Palaeolithic people were already significant farmers, what should we make of the Neolithic Revolution?

CHAPTER 3

....

The Neolithic Revolution

The Neolithic Revolution really was striking. For the first time, in the Middle East around 10,000 years ago, there is unequivocal evidence of cultivation. It is not that caches of grain are found in large quantities: such grain might be gathered, after all. It is that the grain clearly differs from the wild ancestral forms; for example, the seeds are bigger than in the wild. Later comes clear evidence of animal domestication. This time the bones of the butchered animals are smaller than in the wild. The first pastoralists presumably selected the smaller beasts because they were easier to handle – but also perhaps fed them badly, with the result that they could not realize their full genetic potential. At roughly the same time, other changes become evident in the wild environment. In particular other species that were hitherto local, common, and presumably hunted, disappeared. In the Middle East such creatures included fallow deer and gazelles. At about the same time, too, the first permanent, stone-built cities started to appear: Catal Huyuk in Turkey, and Jericho on the West Bank of the Jordan. The picture seems unequivocal, neat and satisfying. People who previously were hunter-gatherers became agricultural, and in the wake of agriculture came the first cities.

But people who study fossils – palaeontologists – emphasize that fossilization is a very rare event. They take it as read that if they find a fossil of any creature then the chances are that that creature was common, which means that it had already been around for a very long time.

The same is true of people who study more recent artefacts – archaeologists. They acknowledge that the chances of any artifact surviving for more than a few years in recognizable form are remote. So if archaeologists do find clear signs of ancient human activity they can infer that the activity had already been practised for a long time, over a wide area. In other words, when the first unequivocal signs of agriculture appear in the Neolithic Revolution, it is reasonable to assume that agriculture was already well established.

The standards that archaeologists set in interpreting signs of ancient agriculture are quite rightly stringent: unless we are stringent, we can never be certain of anything. But the kind of evidence we are looking for would necessarily remain elusive. I am suggesting that Palaeolithic people were managing the flora and the fauna in ways that made a very significant difference to their own ecological success and to the ecology of the creatures around them, but without doing anything on a large scale and without changing the creatures they were affecting in ways that would show up in the archaeological record. Agriculture was an ancient pursuit by the time of the Neolithic Revolution and one that had already made a crucial difference to the ecological success of *Homo sapiens*, and to the ecological collapse of other large mammals that got in their way – including, perhaps, *Homo neanderthalensis*.

What we see in the Neolithic Revolution, then, is not the beginning of agriculture. It is the beginning of agriculture that was being practised on a large scale, in one place, for long periods; and it was already intensive enough to cause physical changes in the crop plants, and later in animals. It was, in short, the kind of agriculture that could promote the growth of cities and of all that goes with civilization.

The same must have been true in principle for all the later outbreaks of agriculture in other parts of the world at later times: in the Indus Valley and China, and at various places in the Americas. Agriculture was not arising afresh in each case. Rather, in different places, at different times, circumstances were such that people started to practise agriculture on a large scale. No instruction manual was being passed from place to place, in a global game of Chinese whispers. Neither need we envisage Neolithic or Palaeolithic anticipations of the Ministry of Agriculture's extension workers. Still less should we entertain some weird quasi-mystical concept of human evolution, envisaging that the ability to farm is a 'stage' that human beings are somehow predestined to achieve.

So now we can ask: What precipitated the practice of agriculture on a large scale in the Middle East 10,000 years ago – and at other places at intervals afterwards? To answer this we must first consider the general features of agriculture, common to all the diverse areas.

General reasons for large-scale agriculture

First, we have to assume that when people practise agriculture, even as a hobby, their population rises above the level that would otherwise be possible. The reason is fundamental. Hunters and gatherers take from their environment only what their environment happens to produce: and if they take too much, the desirable prey species collapse. Their food supply is limited by circumstances beyond their control, and their population ultimately depends upon their food supply.

But the whole point of agriculture is to manipulate the environment so as to increase the amount of food that it will provide. If you fertilize the soil then you increase the total biomass. But even if you do not officiously fertilize, you can increase the output of desirable plants and animals by reducing competition from the less desirable ones – in other words by crop protection, including weeding. And if you increase the food supply, you can increase your own population.

But then, of course, the farmers find themselves in a vicious spiral. The more they farm, the more their population rises and the more they are obliged to farm, because only by farming can they feed the extra mouths.

But in practice the spiral is even more vicious than is immediately obvious. Hunting results in rapidly diminishing returns – it is a risky, arduous and time-consuming business. This is reflected in the fact that predatory animals tend to be spectacularly lazy. Lions, for example, sleep or doze for at least twenty hours a day, and spend another two hours growling and grooming. They hunt for only about two hours a day. Kalahari bushmen have similarly been shown to hunt for only about six hours a week. 'Laziness' is a way of life for the big predator.

But farming changes the rules of the game. Farming manipulates the environment with the express purpose of overcoming its natural restraints. The more you manipulate, the more food you can produce. The harder the farmers work the more food they can produce. Laziness emphatically is not favoured. A hunter who works twice as hard as average may get twice as much food in the short term, but will soon come unstuck as his prey disappears. But the farmer who works ten times as hard as his neighbour will indeed produce ten times as much food – and in favourable circumstances can sustain this tenfold increase indefinitely. Ten times more food means an even greater opportunity for population growth.

Hence the vicious spiral is doubly vicious. The more people farm, the more the population rises and so the more they need to farm. But also, in farming – in sharp contrast to hunting – increased effort does bring increased rewards, with the result that the whole process is accelerated.

However unpleasant agriculture may be, once it becomes large-scale there is no turning back. I have suggested that for many thousands of years people farmed as hobbyists, perhaps taking up farming for a few years in a particular place, and then dropping it, and picking up again elsewhere. I have also suggested that hobby-farmers can be more effective hunters than those who rely entirely upon hunting, because their numbers are no longer controlled so tightly by the prey base.

But people cannot go on farming, and increasing their population, and attacking the wild creatures around them, without having a huge impact. Indeed I have suggested that the Pleistocene overkill may have come about at least in part because the killers were also farmers – and that this in the end is why the Neanderthals lost out.

But, of course, once the wild fauna has collapsed – leaving only the creatures that for one reason or another are able to co-exist with hunting-farming people – living by hunting becomes even less of an option. What little there is left to hunt is especially elusive – like the wandering moose of North America. Farming again becomes less of a hobby and more of a necessity. The loss of fallow deer and gazelle in the Middle East was, perhaps, the equivalent of the North American overkill – except that the Middle Eastern species merely moved elsewhere rather than going extinct.

So we have seen that, once begun, farming obliges people to farm even more, as their populations rise and the wild creatures suffer, eventually to collapse to a new and greatly impoverished level. The farmers do not increase their efforts because they enjoy it, or because it is necessarily easier than hunting and gathering. They are simply the victims of their own success.

Given this build-up, the adoption of large-scale agriculture might seem to have been inevitable. But we can also ask what particular local conditions prompted agriculture to become conspicuous and prevalent in place after place, in a wave of Neolithic revolutions. What those local conditions were, in each case, we can only guess. But the fertile Middle East, where the first of the Neolithic revolutions took place, also provides some of the most fertile ground for speculation.

Special circumstances: Eden and the Ice Age

The first unequivocal intimation of farming that the archaeological record provides is from the Middle East of around 10,000 years ago. So what was happening then to have caused such a jolt in the culture?

Answer: the latest Ice Age was coming to an end. We are used to the notion that Ice Ages are studied by geologists, while the lives of modern human beings – and these were modern people – are the province of archaeologists and historians. But in the Middle East, 10,000 years ago, the three disciplines converge.

It was not that the climate became warmer. That is no obvious reason in itself to increase the intensity of agriculture. We might even argue the reverse, for an improvement in climate might be expected to increase the variety of species to prey upon.

The crucial factor is what happened to the sea. During Ice Ages any water that falls on to land stays there. Huge tracts of North America were under ice that in places was several miles deep. So much water is locked on land that the sea level falls by up to 200 metres. During the most recent Ice Age, Beringia – the land bridge between Alaska and Siberia – was as large as Poland. That is how people crossed from one continent to the other – together with the elk, moose and bison that are now the principal large ungulates in North America. During the most recent Ice Age, too, the great shallow sea that now lies between Saudi Arabia and Iran was not there; the present-day Persian Gulf was dry land.

And the land in what is now the Persian Gulf must have been a very favoured spot, where the Tigris and the Euphrates, which now define Mesopotamia alias Iraq, would have flowed together, and out into the Arabian Sea. The land was flat and the climate balmy. There was no shortage of water. There would have been fish and shellfish galore, and great flocks of water birds, with gazelles and fallow deer and fruiting trees. This would have been the place where the people congregated. I am told that Cape York in northern Australia offered just such an environment for early Aborigines, and indeed still does so. The traditional, modern view of the hunter-gatherer, clinging to existence in some desert or hostile forest, does not apply. You or I, though we may be ultra-urbanized, could easily survive in such places. And the people of the Late Palaeolithic, professional exploiters of the great outdoors, would have lived as if in Paradise. They could have cultivated here and there, as they chose: groves of favoured fruiting trees, a little horticulture, perhaps a little manipulation of the shallows to encourage the fish and shellfish.

But as the Ice Age ended the sea flooded in, swollen by the melting mountains of ice on the continents of the north and the deep south. It came in quickly, furthermore, perhaps in just a few decades. The people, hordes of them, were obliged to move inland to what then was uplands. The population of what had been the coastal plain was already high, the product of a naturally generous environment, and boosted further by hobby farming. But now they all had to crowd into a much smaller space and were obliged to farm to support the augmented population, where before they had farmed just to exercise a little control, and smooth over the seasons.

Their new environment did, however, offer some tremendous compensations. In particular, grasses of the kind known as barley and wheat grew wild on the hills (and oats and rye were probably present too). These crops were easy to gather, and particularly amenable to cultivation. In addition, wheat soon underwent a genetic shift that changed it almost instantly from the wild to the domestic state. In wild wheat the ripe grain is held only precariously to the stem, so that as the autumn winds shake the heads the seeds fall off and are scattered. But in cultivated wheat the seeds are held firmly on the heads until they are beaten off by threshing. The change from one to the other is one of the signs by which archaeologists can see that caches of ancient wheat have been cultivated rather than gathered. After all, plants that held the grain firmly to the stem when the wind blew would not do well in the wild, since their seeds would never be dispersed. This is a largely self-selecting process. The easy way to gather grain *en masse* is to cut the stems – not to remove the seeds individually. But if early gatherers collected wild grain by cutting stems, they would be bound to collect more seed from the stems that held the seeds more firmly. These, then – after threshing – would be the ones they planted.

So the first full-time farmers of the Middle East did enjoy some wonderful serendipity: extremely compliant crops (which indeed have never been surpassed – for wheat is still the world's most abundant crop) and fertile soil in which to grow them. And wheat, of course, and other cereals, are the prime crops of arable farming: crops that are sown in bulk by breaking the soil and scattering the seed. Apart from rice, in the Far East, cereals are not generally sown plant by plant, as in horticulture. So it is reasonable to suggest that the Neolithic Revolution, though not the beginning of farming *per se*, represents the beginning of bona fide arable farming. And of course, once arable farming was established it was extremely productive. Nowadays a field of wheat yields at least ten times as many edible calories or protein as the same area devoted, say, to grazing livestock; and we need not suppose that the ratio would have been very different in earliest times. In short, arable farming got under way when it did, in the Middle East at least, thanks to two serendipitous discoveries: the most compliant crop species in the world, and a particularly favoured terrain. Everything was propitious.

An American scholar, Juris Zarins of the University of Missouri, has suggested that the flooding of the Persian Gulf and the subsequent events underpin the story of the Garden of Eden, so beautifully recorded in Genesis; and I find this thesis eminently plausible. Of course it has often been suggested that the end of Eden represents a folk memory of hunting and gathering, when life was easy. But Zarins is far more specific. He points out that Genesis (2:10–14) meticulously describes where Eden was:

> And a river went out of Eden to water the garden; and from thence it was parted, and became into four heads.
> The name of the first is Pison: that is it which compasseth the whole land of Havilah, where there is gold;
> And the gold of that land is good there is bdellium and the onyx stone.
> And the name of the second river is Gihon: the same is it that compasseth the whole land of Ethiopia.

And the name of the third river is Hiddekel; that is it
which goeth towards the east of Assyria. And the fourth
river is Euphrates.

Zarins now does a little geographical speculation. Havi-
lah is in the south-west of Mesopotamia: gold was indeed
mined there, and the aromatic resin bdellium can still be
found. The Pison could be the present-day Wadi Batin,
which is now a wadi – a dried river bed. 'Ethiopia' is
probably a mistranslation, and more than likely refers to
an area of south-east Mesopotamia, in which case Gihon
could be the present-day Karun. The Karun has now
been dammed but at one time it carried most of the
sediment out of the highlands of Iran to form the delta
of the modern Persian Gulf. Hiddekel is the Tigris, and
the Euphrates is the Euphrates. Trace these four rivers
back and they converge at a spot that now lies several
kilometres off shore in the Persian Gulf.

As we have seen, 8,000 years ago a great deal of the
Persian Gulf was still dry land. This great, flat, bountiful
plain was not hypothetical. It was real, and glorious, and
remembered. Of course, Genesis was probably written
about 1500 BC and the events that are being remembered
probably occurred about 4,500 years before that, so the
memory is indeed ancient. But that is not at all implau-
sible. There is no reason why folk memories – even in
the absence of the written word – should not persist
effectively forever. Australian aborigines have memories
of places that were flooded 8,000 years ago just as the
Persian Gulf had been; and when modern divers go to

look they find the features far beneath the waves, precisely as described.

The sheer awfulness of farming

The traditional view of farming's origins – the picture I somewhat parodied at the beginning of this book – suggests that hunting and gathering was hard, and that farming is fundamentally easy, so that once farming was discovered people naturally took to it. The evidence is totally to the contrary. A life of hunting and gathering, particularly in favoured places like the ancient Persian Gulf and Cape York, can be easy and agreeable, not to say fun. These Neolithic people did not embark on a life of arable farming because they wanted to, or because they saw the advantages of cereals. They did it because they were forced into it when their paradise was taken from them and they were shoved together into hills that just turned out to be especially hospitable. Arable farming is seasonal, but in the season it is hell; and the treatment of the grain after harvest, in threshing and milling, is at least as hard as the work before. Most of the Old Testament is about early arable farming – although not particularly early, because farming had been practised for several thousand years by the time the accounts were written. The Old Testament can in fact be read like a bumper edition of *The Farmer's Weekly*, and the stories it tells are horrendous: of famines, of slave labour, and of unremitting toil. Look, for instance, at the story of Ruth gleaning, picking up the fallen seed (for this was still primitive corn, still liable to fall off the stem) after the sicklers have been. The grind of farming by hand was beautifully described only one hundred years ago by Leo Tolstoy in *Anna Karenina*: the sheer physical effort of wielding a scythe, hour after hour. And if you don't do it at the appointed time, then you lose the crop, and starve. Even now you can just watch any South-East Asian farmer ploughing a monsoon field with a bullock-plough. The labour is horrendous. Yet the first arable farmers did not even have bullocks to help them along or beautiful iron scythes. They had sickles.

There is archaeological evidence, too, of disease and trauma from early arable days that is not seen in earlier, hunting people. Thus Theya Molleson of the Natural History Museum in London has described a characteristic syndrome in which the toes and knees are bent and arthritic and the lower back is deformed – a syndrome that she has very plausibly traced to the use of the saddle quern, in which the grain was ground into flour after harvesting. Later querns were revolved, which can be done in the way that a sailor turns a capstan – and could be turned by animal power or, later, by water or wind power. But primitive saddle querns were simply shoved to and fro, a horrendous task. Wheat and barley are less forgiving than rice, in that they do need to be ground before eating.

So the people of the Middle East emphatically did not become arable farmers because it was better or easier. They did it because they were forced into it: first for the general reason that the more they farmed the more they needed to farm, as their populations increased — the vicious spiral; and second for the specific reason that as the seas rose they lost their wonderful hunting ground. The existence of wheat and barley, and of soil to grow them in, made the transition possible.

But they didn't like it. Indeed we can reasonably guess that they hated it. In fact, Genesis says as much. For as God banishes Adam and Eve from the Garden of Eden he curses them (Genesis 3:19): 'In the sweat of thy face shall thou eat bread, till thou return unto the ground.' That, at least, is the King James version. It is an awful phrase — 'In the sweat of thy face': much more powerful than 'the sweat of your brow', as the phrase tends to be translated in some other versions. It has the provocative, aggressive quality of the modern American expression 'Get out of my face!' The meaning is unmistakable. To condemn all of humankind to a life of full-time farming, and in particular of arable farming, was a curse indeed.

Why did other peoples farm?

So what were the local conditions that prompted other peoples to become conspicuous farmers in other places, at later times? In China, the Indus Valley, the Americas and the Pacific? The answer is I don't know. But at least we know what we should be looking for: on the one hand, rising population pressure and declining fauna, obliging the people to rely more and more on their own cultivations; and on the other hand, opportunity.

If people are to make the transition to arable farming, as opposed to *ad hoc* horticulture, they need a suitable crop to cultivate. The big-seeded grasses – cereals – of the Middle East are wonderful, supreme. Rice filled the same role in eastern Asia. The people of the Americas found another big-seeded grass, *Zea*, which, when cultivated, becomes maize. In the south the first Americans found two more grain crops that were not grasses: seeds of *Amaranthus*, alias amaranth; and of *Chenopodium*, alias quinoa. Other chenopodiums also featured as both grain crops and green crops in Iron Age Europe, notably Fat Hen and Good King Henry. It would be fun (if somewhat pointless) to breed Fat Hen into a decent crop, and develop a cuisine based on it. The South Americans also discovered and developed the world's most important tuber, the potato, though first (and still) they had to cope with its often fearsome toxicity. And there are many others: pulses, squashes, chocolate, and so on. Overall then, there is no shortage of good potential crop plants in America that lend themselves to arable techniques or to mass horticulture. But you have to discover them first.

Most early farmers managed to acquire at least some domestic livestock as well. This too requires serendipity, for not all creatures lend themselves easily to domestication. Animals whose habits are solitary or are too big, fierce or swift, or are given to migration, generally do not make good domesticates. Only now, with the aid of wire fencing and four-wheel-drive vehicles, are farmers finding it reasonably possible to farm red deer, for instance, which are just too swift and skittish. The people of the Middle East, however, found on hand sheep and goats – both of which are small and relatively easy to control. Lead one and you can lead them all. The earliest South American farmers found the four native Camelids – llamas, alpacas, guanacos and vicunas – similarly accommodating. Many other animals scavenged from human settlements – dogs and pigs very probably found a symbiotic relationship with human beings long before people settled as farmers. Dogs oblige by eating human faeces; in context, they are creatures of hygiene. Small creatures could be caught and enclosed. Thus Neolithic people probably enclosed rabbits, and South Americans soon developed a cuisine for guinea-pig.

Archaeologists have traditionally seen the domestication of livestock animals as a steady encroachment on their wildness; first lying in wait for them; then following them, as the Lapps still follow the reindeer herds; then directing them to particular places that were most convenient to the hunter, not least by the use of fire, as practised by Australian aborigines; then coralling; then controlling their reproduction, which leads on to selective breeding. This in general must have been how things went. Perhaps it is wrong, though, to see this just as increasing domination or 'dominion', as Genesis has it. As Stephen Budiansky points out in *Covenant of the Wild*, the animals that did lend themselves to domestication were given protection and food, and therefore were able to breed more successfully than those who remained in the wild. To a large extent an animal's aptitude for domestication is under genetic control. Some creatures, like dogs and sheep, domesticate very easily while others, such as gazelles, do not; and within any one species some individuals are more suited temperamentally to domestication than others. Anyone who has ever kept any kind of domestic animal knows that this is true: their personalities differ enormously, and while some are placid others always retain their freedom of spirit. (Many tomcats are 'domestic' only in the loosest sense.)

Thus, as Budiansky argues, genes that produced placidity and homeliness would spread, once human beings provided conditions that favoured those qualities. So although domestication may seem undignified, it is good for the genes that predispose an organism to it. Hence, in a world run by humans, a predilection for domesticity can be good for the animals too. Certainly those that have become domestic are far more numerous than their relatives who have stuck to the wild. Modern domestic cattle are as common as mice (at least as wild mice) while most species of wild cattle are on their beam-ends and several have become extinct. Hence, as Budiansky says, domestication can be seen not as domination but as a 'covenant'.

No-one could begin full-time farming, and in particular arable farming, just anywhere. Or at least if they did, they could not expect to continue doing so for very long. For in the absence of modern cultivations and methods of soil improvement – or even with such advantages, in many places – full-time farming, and especially arable farming, cannot generally be sustained.

Only a few places are moist enough and fertile enough to allow continued depradations: places like, say, Hertfordshire, and other infinitely forgiving fields of Northern Europe, where there is plenty of rain and the sun is not too fierce. Thus, farming appeared only spottily here and there in the millennia after the Neolithic Revolution of the Middle East, because in the beginning there were only relatively few places where it could be practised on a large scale over a reasonable period of time. In the absence of modern farming techniques, few places can sustain stable agriculture.

In other places – that is, over much of the world – the activity that we northern Europeans call 'farming' just won't work, or at least not for long. Thus in Imperial vein former scholars were wont to conclude that Australian aborigines did not farm in European style because they were 'backward'. The assumption is that they would have got round to it sooner or later even if Europeans had not arrived and shown them how. Nonsense. The first Australians did not farm Australia in the manner of Europe because that would have been an immensely foolish thing to do. Much of Australia is desert or tropical forest, and even much of the coastal strip is subject to prolonged droughts. It is difficult, too, to identify any native Australian plant that would lend itself to cultivation in the manner of, say, wheat, rice or squashes. But, as we have seen, the native Australians do practise 'firestick farming' and in New South Wales they did traditionally dam the rivers to husband the fish and shellfish. They are, in fact, expert managers of land and game; and in that environment, their more hands-off methods are highly appropriate, not to say wonderful.

To be sure, European farming has been made to succeed in various areas of Australia. After all, Australia is a vast country with many micro-habitats – and 'micro' in Australia is big by European standards. But European-style agriculture insouciantly applied has also created some spectacular deserts, to add to what was there before; and such bullish agriculture could not have got under way unless aided by the technique, wealth, and ruthless will of Europe. It is almost inconceivable that Eurasian-style agriculture could ever have grown up in Australia without help from outside. It's not that kind of country; nor does it have appropriate potential crops. The first Australians could not have been ignorant of the techniques, however. After all, Australia was joined to New Guinea at the time that the Persian Gulf was dry land. The people of New Guinea at that time were already perfectly good horticulturalists. But Australia was a place to be managed, rather than gardened.

CONCLUSION

....

Human beings manipulated their environment to some extent, to their own advantage, even before they were bona fide human beings. These manipulations graded into farming by a series of minute steps, and fitfully. Palaeontologists and archaeologists have described a particularly striking watershed around 40,000 years ago, when the anatomically modern human beings, *Homo sapiens*, seemed truly to get into their stride. So it seems reasonable to suggest that this is when true farming began as well — many millennia before the Neolithic Revolution.

Farming eventually succeeded, ecologically speaking, not because it is pleasant but because it works: it coaxes more food from the environment than would otherwise be the case. Because of this, it enables human populations to rise; and it favours people who work hard whereas hunters — human or animal — are not rewarded for their efforts in the same way. Large populations of hard-working people will inevitably prevail over smaller populations of people who are more laid-back.

The Neolithic Revolution does not represent the

beginning of farming. It does represent the transition between hobby farming – a supplement to hunting and gathering – and the time when, prompted by changing circumstances and necessity, farming became the norm. Ever since that time the human population has been rising exponentially, from an estimated eight million worldwide around 10,000 years ago, to between one hundred and three hundred million at the time of Christ, to six billion – 6,000 million – by 2000 AD.

But now we must wonder how much longer this exponential rise can continue. More generally it is time to ask whether the policy of bullishness and hard work that is symbolized by Cain's murder of Abel, and brought such success to the Neolithic farmers and their successors, will be appropriate for very much longer. Our earliest hunting ancestors must have been lazy, as lions are. Perhaps we should learn from them.

REFERENCES AND ACKNOWLEDGEMENTS
....

The main ideas in this book have largely been acquired informally – through conversations over several decades. Not all of my mentors and informants have written easily available books or articles. It seems appropriate, therefore, simply to record my thanks to the people of whose help I am most conscious (though emphasizing that they should not be held responsible for my own eccentricities); and to invite you to look out for their work.

For ideas on **human evolution** in general I am particularly grateful to: Roger Lewin, who has written some of the clearest and most comprehensive accounts of human evolution, sometimes in collaboration with Richard Leakey; Chris Stringer, of London's Natural History Museum, who has recently co-authored popular books with Clive Gamble (*In Search of the Neanderthals*, Thames and Hudson, 1993) and with Robin McKie; and Bernard Wood, now at the George Washington University, who frequently writes comment pieces for *Nature*.

For views on early **human ecology and economics** I am beholden to: Rob Foley at the University of

Cambridge (see, for example, *Another Unique Species*, Longman, 1987); and Clive Gamble, University of Southampton (see his book, *In Search of the Neanderthals*, with Chris Stringer, mentioned above).

For ideas on the emergence of **agriculture**, and on the true nature of agriculture, I am most conscious of my debt to: John Yellen, National Science Foundation, Washington, who first suggested to me that late Palaeolithic people were 'farming' up to a point, and that Hottentots had a take-it-or-leave-it attitude to animal husbandry; Rhys Jones, Australian National University, Canberra, who coined the expression 'firestick farming' and first showed me that there is more to land and game management than growing corn; David Harris, of the Institute of Archaeology, University College London, who edited *The Origins and Spread of Agriculture and Pastoralism in Eurasia* (UCL Press, 1996); Mark Nesbitt, University College London, a leading authority on the Neolithic Revolution; Theya Molleson of the Natural History Museum, who has revealed the pathologies of early Egyptian farmers and food processors; E. R. Orskov, of the Rowett Research Institute, Aberdeen, whose overview of livestock farming worldwide is second to none; and Paul Richards, of University College London, whose studies of traditional African farmers – seeing the inventiveness behind the apparent conservatism – is revelatory.

The notion of the **Pleistocene overkill**, which plays a large part in this book, has been propounded mainly by Paul S. Martin of the University of Arizona in

Tucson. Among my most valued volumes is the book he co-edited with Richard G. Klein, now at the University of Chicago, *Quarternary Extinctions: A Prehistoric Revolution* (University of Arizona Press, 1984).

For a sense of how **geological change** affects people's lives, see *Tales of the Earth: Paroxysms and Perturbations of the Blue Planet* by Charles Officer and Jake Page (Oxford University Press, 1993).

Finally, try reading the Bible, and in particular Genesis and Exodus (and most of the rest, including the New Testament parables) not simply as a work of religion or literature, but as an account of early farming and of what it meant to people. Such an approach is most illuminating!